# DUEL

by Brianna Florian
with attributions from
Gia Florian
and
Dale Florian

Hilary,

I really enjoy your presence and your aura. Thank you for joining me on the first week journey as an Optimystic P-Head. Thank you for openly sharing your stories. You've got an amazing tool box and you have inspired me to be a great mother.

xoxox Brianna

# Part 1:
# The Shallows

In a time when I needed help but only had a rhyme, a pen and paper... I let the words flow when I was feeling low. But, who wants a book full of depression?

I read my words and engaged the light within, to channel the messages I needed to hear, the ones that made it all clear.

Now I look back as a reminder of where I was and how I've grown. Yet, the messages still have the same depth now as when I wrote them.

Each page requires you to read from a new point of view.

xoxox

# Lens of Child

Hi, I'm eleven years old
Your future is in my hands
The education I receive can make or break me, us, the world

Being in a box with fluorescent light hurts my brain
Being told to hush hurts my heart
Being expected to sit 8 hours a day hurts my health
Being taught a false history messes with my perception

I can't choose my life now; I'm only eleven
You can make a difference for the both of us, all of us
You can love me
You can spend time with me
You can teach me through your stories
You can bring me to the park to engage with other children
You can let me bang on the counters and scream melodies
You can show me the world

Together we can be an unstoppable force
I know your heart; I know what you missed in your life
I am you; I am your seed

Plant me in the richest soil
Water me with pure water
Give me sunlight
Speak kind words to me as I grow

I will bloom for you, for our family, for the world

## Lens of Elder

Hello, I am ninety-five years old
Your future is in my hands
When this body dies, my Spirit will guide you

I know Western education dumbs you down
I know you are exhausted and restless
I know your day dreams and night mares
I have always been there and will always stay

I cannot choose my life, this body needs me
I can choose when this body dies
I choose to be with you, young one
To experience a life through your eyes
When the going gets tough, think of me
I will light your path
I will whisper secrets in your ears
I will show you the universe
Let go and live through my Spirit

Together we are unstoppable
I am your heart, mind and soul
I will water you and watch you grow

Your radiance will be forever known
When it is time, lay under the stone
And come back Home

## War

Please throw your perspectives in a grenade
I'll catch that mother fucker
Light myself on fire
To return from my ashes
Stronger than before

I'll stack your boxes into a pyramid
Climb to the top; SHINE
I may be losing my mind...
You can call this perspective The Luxor

## Love

To each their own
Know your zone
Find a clone
Never again alone. .

H O M E
Where love trumps all
Send it to receive it
Watch worlds transform before you

## High Walls

What is it like to know Love?

It is claustrophobia
It is the last breath of air before insanity
It is the last clean river for drinking
It is the last ice berg slowly melting
It is the fire consuming everything I once had; I once knew

I know love...I feel its suffering
I long for its joy
I long for the light of love

Ego addicted to suffering
What else does it know?

Protect the heart. Protect it with everything you've got

Build a wall so high, not even these words can transcend it...

# Higher Ambition

You know Love
You never lost it, but rejected it

Your wall is your lack of imagination
Now cut the shit and paint it!

Ego is but energy all beings feel
The part of Ego you choose could make or break your future

Forget the suffering, you do not deserve that
You are blessed with light, love and health

Be the change you wish to see
Open your Eye
See through the wall
And you will find Us

We've been waiting
Sending all of our love to sit atop your wall
We know your ambition can transcend it

Now fly over, young one
See the sights beyond fears
Always know that We are near

## Feed Me

Piss me off
Make me feel the fire in the belly of the dragon
Don't dare think you can steal the light of the princess in the
castle

I love when you remind me of the darkness I dwell in

Throw your stones
I'll add those to my collection
I'm building a bigger castle

## Love Me

Bri, Bri, let down your hair
Can you hear my boom box playing In Your Eyes?
I've been waiting outside your window
Throwing rocks in hopes you will notice my approach

I. Love. You.
Where are you?
Jump out of that castle, my love
Diminishing Dragon's everlasting wrath
Settle the fire in the belly
        Tame it.
Don't allow fame to claim it.
You can have my attention...

# Who am I?

Not feeling Brianna; feeling Him
Making choices that hurt
They cut deep
A large watermelon sliced in half
Emotion evaporating
Each water droplet a decision disappearing in air
Effect unseen...felt
Is our love evaporating with each path I travel?
What a heavy weight mind carries
Effects of my forcefulness
Rationality chased our lost love
Decreased the rate at which we could reconnect
To face my decisions, face my regrets, face my reflection
Fear and blockages arise
A mini of my mother's arrogance
Every idea of her that I hate, I cannot face in myself....
Apologies only go so far
Do I stay in this world of illusion?
Do I back out and pray for you?
Would you come if I never stepped another foot; would you turn around for me?
Only limitations between us
I pray I break these walls without breaking your heart
Or have I already ripped it apart?
Burry the pieces then dig them up
Losing the nerves to the earth's pull
Will there be anything left of you when I return home?
What is humility?
What does it feel like?
Sit silent in the roller coaster of mind
Speak aloud risking reckless foolishness
Balance two aspects into One
We are One; my walls separate us
Please wait as I climb over to the greener grass

## You Are You

I never left your side, Brianna
You lost your sight
Now that you've seen me,
You've taken flight

I am always in your Heart
As you are always in mine
Our connection is a cord of the strongest energy
Remember this when you sleep without me

I could never leave you behind
You could never break my heart
We are the first beam of light
You are mine; I am yours
You are the One I adore

Remember, space is a word created
We know nothing of space
Connection is Truth
Let go of fears
Let love carry us through the galaxies
This is our magic carpet ride

# YOU A BITCH

I'd beat your fucking ass…
But you a little bitch boy
And I ain't tryna pay your medicals,
After I knock all your teeth out

I've been waiting to round house kick a mother fucker in the jaw

Real sly you think you are
I know you're a psychopath
Who do you think you're fooling?
Damn, I thought I was crazy
            HA!

Real funny you think you are
No damn body is laughing at your jokes tho…
Keep your mouth shut
Before I stuff it with my fist

Real tough you think you are
Until this five foot female whoops your ass
Call me Ma Ma before I knock your lights out

Wait, you have no light
Yours burned out a while ago
Back to the darkness you go…

And have a blessed day

### Sho' Am

Can't touch this BriBriiiiiii
Try to round house kick me...
I'll stiff arm you, put you to sleep
#stillsleepin

But I respect you for trying . . .

## Marry Me

You calm the tornado of my mind
I settle down when your smile reaches mine
Other men want this Divine Light
I want to focus on you as if you are my last right...

We don't need to get married
But, put a ring on this finger
Let's explore what it feels like

A place where mistakes are accepted
Right is wrong....

Deep down I know all along; you are the one
You understand this mess around my head
Darling, you are my sun in this storm

## When It's Time

I would LOVE to marry you
When the time is right...

You've got a lot to learn
A light to ignite

What we have, you are not ready for
When you are ready there will be NOTHING in between us

Keep your head up
Keep our love in your heart
Keep a picture of me in your mind

Add my last name to your first
Visualize our marriage

I will do all the same

## Repulsed By Men

To the men that look with that smirk
Their eyes say they only see vagina

Step closer and notice I haven't shaved in two months
Take a whiff of my cigarette breath
Still want inside this vagina?

To the men that yell out their window "you are beautiful"
Asking if I like men

Yes, I like men; men that have enough respect to get the fuck
out of their car when they see a beautiful woman

Men that arouse my mind before arousing my body
Men that see soul before their penis jumps for vagina
The thought of "fucking" repulses me
A piñata beaten until his nectar releases
To hell with those men

My vagina is sacred
My lips are scared
My time is sacred

Treat me as a queen if you wish to partake in my Divine Light

## Mommy Issues

To the women who ignore my smile
FUCK YOU
Literally, I will pound your pussy when I get the chance,
because you can't see the pain in my eyes

Yes, I yelled out of my car window...
Cause I'm at a stop light
Fuck you think this is, a Chinese fire drill?

Your mind means nothing to me if you can't return a smile

Momma didn't teach me much
What she did was enough:
A smile is contagious, be the realest illness

Moms wasn't around and pops was a clown
I learned to turn my frown upside down

So baby, yeah you fine
But you ain't Divine

I'll keep this smile of mine

. . .

## Xoxox

Fucking bitch
I said it
Go to hell...
Whoops you are already there

Heaven is a place of love and understanding
I understand you fell far from the tree
Don't put your blame on me
Keep your hate for yourself
I have enough weight on my back

Words sparked the Queen of Hearts
Now, off with your head!

Darkness back in action
Oh wee oh my

Don't steal my light
Strength is hindering
Never one for creative "dis backs"
Life is a joke...right?

I'll collect jokes like I collect hearts
Then shove them up your ass far enough for you to forget who
you are

Call me Hancock
And have a blessed day

## Take Care

Now. Now. Now.
Is that any way to speak to another being?
  K A R M A
Kindly Approach Ridiculous Minds Appropriately

End and begin with love
One Eye, One Mind, One Soul

Get power under control
Watch mold sculpt
Infinite vibrations,
In mind when manifesting schemes and plotting time

## Brand New

I hear you
But, I don't want to
Ignorance was bliss
A simple kiss and I'm back in the mix

Pot of life
Stirring the jungle

Loss of words
Loss of emotions

Words don't matter anyway...

Was chasing fame
Now I see the game
Hope fame never knows my name

Pick a goal
Pick a man
Make a fam
Live in slow motion
No more commotion
No chaos

F R E E

## Slow... Never Been You

HA Ha HA, Bri Bri...
How fresh is the seed of mind?
Swirls in the chaos of all time
What else but turning pain into profit?
Slow lane?
Ain't ever been your thang

Accelerate; master of pace
Spitting rhymes in faces of rabbits

Fame; same as no fame
A huge game
Make that name
& make it BIG

## Sleep With You

Yes I want to sleep with you
On my terms...
Yes I want your dick in my vagina
On my terms...

What are my terms?
They are simple

Stay still and look into my eyes
Feel the power of this energy field
Travel to another world within me
Leave the pains of this one behind
No pounding this pussy...
Your pains will melt away with still pleasure

Let my mind be your treasure chest
Open me up then lay me to rest

### Sleep Within You

Babe, I GET IT
You wanna travel through the realms
While your vagina devours my dick
That's cool and all, but...
Let's live in THIS moment
Forget those other worlds

Now is OUR time to shine; stars aligned
Set the night sky on fire
Others will travel to our world to feel a love so strong
God may have went wrong bringing us together
We'll be lucky if we ever make it through a night like this
No need for material bliss

We can be "still" when we are dead

## I Should Keep My Big Mouth Shut

I'm sorry universe
Please forgive this Ego
Please understand
I'll do my best to keep my Truths to myself
Or present them in the form of a vague question
I want to return to the Light
If only Ego would release its pain

Who could I be when Ego works with me?

## Open Your Big Eye

Seedling of a never ending string
All come back to Me
One by One

Forgive yourself
Love yourself

I created Ego
There is nothing to be ashamed of

Work with what you've got
I've given it to you...

Be grateful
Be humble

You are the Light
You never left

## Self Love

What a trickster self love has been
Billions of hobbies in this world
Where does God want me?
I choose...insanity
Every shade of black swirls above
A beautiful fog
Fixate my gaze on the Yellow Brick Road

Heart torn apart
Spread wide and far
Don't push my brain...
It's close to the edge
The courage to move on
No motivation to move up

Desires burning holes in worn clothes
Naked when they found me
Floating on this dark cloud
Afraid of the come down

Let One in, they whisper
How do I choose?
When I'm afraid to lose...

## Shared Love

Pick yo poison
Fight yo battles
Do you, boo boo

Loose screws turn to the right, to the right
What you need tightened will turn to the right

Many faces along the path
Few will follow
Lead them through darkness with your Vision
Each hold a piece of your heart
Torn apart to reconnect

No need to climb when you are already on top

He is the one you love
He is the one you need
He is the only one you see

Put his love on top
& be free

## Where's My Man

His smile lights the building
His words dance in my dreams
His hands all over this body
His eyes are galaxies beyond imagination

What we've got we keep quiet
The love speaks for itself

He is dismembered in my heart
Bits and pieces here and there
He is everywhere

All he wants; the loyalty that has left my being
Lost in lust
Love, a feeling I've forgotten...

**I Been Here**

…waiting….patiently…..

I got what you need
But you say I'm just a friend

Let me in
Love will never be forgotten once it is Truthfully felt

## Open My Gate

Cannot forget you
Mesmerized by your eyes
Your talent, your words

I never had you, but you were always mine
Maybe in time our hearts will rhyme

The gate keeper of my ice berg is warming to your touch
You are putting spells in her mind
Over time, I will be yours

Wait patiently for the gate code, please and thank you

## I've Stopped Knocking

My love left when you hid the code
Patience as thin as ice in 2017
As cold as the feeling of you letting me walk away...

No spell can save you from the hell you've created

Body suits matching every mask
A mask for every new face you meet

Keeping these words on the low
Softly whispering them to you
In hopes time will mend your scattered mind

## Alone

I am breathing, yet my heart stopped beating
Left identity with a thief of love
My soul darkened; I fought the pain
What was left to live for?
A spec of light in my core
A spec of myself begging for more
Don't give up; he's out there waiting
That little voice chirped as I kept debating
Pull the trigger, finish this
The ache will end the faster you bend the knuckle

I'm still here
I heard the chirp, listened through the heart throb
I found the bird I wished for upon a shooting star
Was the time wrong, or was my head?
I lay in bed, alone, knowing I have a clone
I can't reach him physically, spiritually or mentally
Chaotic emotions separate us
Where does this leave me?
Alone in my head, fighting the dread

## Loner

There is a difference, you know…

Alone – having no one else present; on one's own
Loner – a person who prefers not to associate with others

You are NEVER alone; God is within
You have wandered where all the loners go
A place in space you call your own
Bubbled by your imagination
A thick wall of perception

Don't let us in…
Don't dare hear our voices; our messages
We watch the game you play
Moving the key hole as if this is Whac-A-Mole

We are always here, my dear
Alone you will never be
A loner you will stay until you can focus on today
Focus on NOW
Jump off that cloud
Watch as you float down
We are all around….
Hear our sounds

Vibrations never lie

## Clearing My Mirror

Knowing the truth and not knowing how to obtain it

Frustration. Confusion. Ego.

Surrender is the way
Surrender to the light

Simple to say; hard to produce
Producing courage to surrender

Wondering what surrender looks like
Feels like, tastes and smells like

Hanging on to a vision
Heavy piece of my fallen mirror
Not knowing where it fell from
Not knowing how to patch it

Not knowing slowly killing Ego
Preparing for my mirror to be clearer than ever

## You Got This, Boo Boo

You can do it!
We believe in you!

Surrender to Truth!

Everything you need is here for you!

Heaven on Earth
Rebirth
Know your worth

Love thyself
Love all
Love God

Move on….
Write a new song
You are where you belong

## Character

I must be a terrible judge of character
Or was it your eyes telling lies?
My perception saw what I wanted you to be
Who I wanted you to be for me

Time to take time to love myself
A lover comes with complications all over my ovaries
No more cock juice for Bri

Spending power on useless wishes
Shedding skin and burying it
To watch the mold grow into a fruit tree
Off of which I will eat

The time is now to cut the ties
Realize who I am inside
Without beating meat
In the back seat
Next to a car seat...

Oh how I will soar
As I stitch these wounds
And color these scars

## Paint Movies

Words and thoughts manifest worlds
Keep shaking that ass, girlllllll;
You'll get exactly what you *assed* for

Visualize without expectations
Open to receiving the gifts
Erase programming; replace with feelings
Leave lost skin in the dust
Move along with grace at a steady pace
With a smile on your face

## Jokester

I am not the typical beautiful woman
I am a jokester
Does that make me more masculine?

I say no.
It was this childhood
I had to stay entertained

Now I've met the jokester and lost my place
Or did I find it...?

## Why So Serious?

You say you're a jokester
You say you have thick skin
You say you take nothing personally

Remember babe, energy speaks louder than words
Your energy swirls with the emotions you carry...

Let that shit go and be merry

## Cute Woman Guilt

The feeling I have when I watch the ice cream man pass the
begging homeless woman
That same ice cream man gives me a free treat every day...

Cute woman guilt
She's no different from I
We are both homeless, hungry, smell like we haven't showered
in days
Both "crazy" talking to ourselves
Both at the park; our only safe space
Both with boobs, ass and vagina
Mine is hairy, maybe hers is too...

Give her an ice cream, light up her world
Give her a reason to smile
A smile she would contain all day

Oh beautiful woman
How I wish I could wipe your pain away
Clean it with the wash rag I carry

Oh beautiful woman
You are light and love
We are different embodiments of the same struggle
Lift yourself beautiful woman
Rise from your ashes

The ice cream man will regret the day he ignored your beauty

## Powerful Woman Privilege

What makes you feel guilty?
BABY, YOU WERE BORN THIS WAY!
Strut your goods, on the runway of Life

Bri, you are fine
Wanna make you mine
I like the way you lick that popsicle….

That other woman cannot do it like you
She doesn't try
Don't feel bad for dried out American Pie

Let her lie under the trees
While you lie with me

Leaders of the New School
Let them hear you…scream

## Analogies

I'm not one for metaphors
When it describes the life I set out for

Manifestation is a tricky spell
I scream my wishes but I can never tell
When they are in front of me..
Maybe I am not ready

Kanye said "no one man should have all that power"

Why do I deserve the book of secrets?
And what do I do to keep it?

I share my truths to you
And they'll only travel to the shallow depths of your mind
I'll give it time as I hide behind the curtains of the mountain you
climb

## Symbols

OK, wicked witch of the west
Careful not to get squashed by a house
I know that's your biggest fear

Come, come my dear
Hideaway in my castle
Dorothy will never find you here

No love spells necessary
I'll lay it on you marvelously every night
Climbing the mountain of your love
A never ending journey
Summon the Wizard on a magic carpet

You've exhausted my Jimmy..

## Hurt So Deep

Hurt so deep I want to disappear in the misery
Never show my face to the public
No need for a name
If only it was easier done than said
What a deep need to feel important
To be known for creative works

How can I let this go when I'm in so deep?
Sinking in muddy emotions
Clenching my arms and legs
Murking chakras
The surface rising above my throat
Spoken word could drown or save me...
What will it be?

## Swim Already

How long do you think you can run?
You are no Usain Bolt

Mind over matter my ass..
Turn the fuck around and face your fears!
Pull the energy into your body
Make shit happen!
Sinking is *only* possible if you forget to swim...

Relax, enjoy the flow
Let go of confusion
Play the game
Live without regrets
SPEAK YOUR MIND!

Focus thoughts into goals
Ask and you shall receive
We're all waiting to give freely

By the way, you can never run from us

## Monumental

Today is monumental
The battle has been won!
Candles of war have burned dim
Mind and soul dwell on the same frequency
At peace, together in infinity

An eternity of imagination
Doodles of the heart flowing within physical reality

Caged eagle set free
Divine light mending broken wings
Scar tissue healing

What a sight to be seen
True colors soaring

## Awareness

Thank God for the days you see the light
Keep shining, Bri Bri
You can do it all; anything you set your mind to
With the right timing and open perception...

Thank God for your exceptional balance
Keep balanced, Bri Bri
You can see both sides of the field
With good intentions, trek onward...

Thank God for your ability to feel and heal
Keep awareness, Bri Bri
You are a voice for the numb
With attention on you, guidance will show you the best moves

## Social Media

Oooooh social media
You're an amazing distraction
A veil over the loneliness
A rose bush in the desert
Social media….
How could you be so beautiful?
Yet sting like a bee
Where are your manners?
Can't you see the chaos you've created?
Can't you see the souls you've stolen?


Give mine back
You can no longer control my Divine Light

## Dear Brianna

. . . . .

Quit acting like you don't *love* Snapchat
Over there making clips instead of moves
Acting as if you don't keep track of your Instagram likes
Acting like you aren't a YouTube Star
Shut the fuck up...
Or go live with the trees

## Thanks Katy Perry

Why must I question my actions?
My actions act upon feelings
Feelings deeper than my mind can grasp
Who am I kidding?
I'm Rose and my feelings are Jack
I could make room to feel
...why do that when it's easier to let go
Let the feelings float away
As I put my rose colored glasses on
And party all night long

## You're Welcome

Brianna, you see
Rose glasses are no distraction from your vision
Party on
& work harder!
You've got the stamina
You've got the Voice
You FEEL
I know it can get chaotic
Those times are the important lessons
From Darkness, you shall grow
Make that money; don't let it make you

## Pain Into Money

Is it arrogant to always find a way to turn pain into money?
A voice justifies the need for security
Spirit whispers I could live without it
Programming seems to think otherwise
The neglect wants to be heard, seen, felt
The struggle wants to hold the cash


The woman wants to pay for everyone
Are their burdens mine?
Could I let them go?

## Congratulations

Make the money; don't let it make you
Sharing is caring
Wealth can bring health

Stack those dollar bills
Then pass them out
Watch the pain disappear
If only for a moment . . .

Now, they all say congratulations

## Leave The Door Open

I got the keys
I got the keys

Would I open the doors?
Fuck yes I will!

Would you keep it open?
For the rest of Me

You see, he and she are parts of Me
One of the same giant masterpiece
Peace be with Us...

I'm the stone thrown
My ripples show
Then slow
Until another stone is thrown

Ripples knocking at doorways
Patience as I find the keys for these new ways
All I ask...
Leave the door open for the rest of Me

## As You Wish

After you, Queen B
Behind you I shall stay
A door stop placed at every new path you encounter
Plenty of Space for the Human Race

Claps to you, Queen B
A beautiful tree you've grown to be
Rooted, grounded, centered, strong
Characteristics of a Leader

Any step you take
       They will follow
Any move you make
       They will follow

A new wave stirring in the Pot of Life
Ride it
When the tide becomes high
Glide above it

Keep shining, Queen B
Let the winning take your time; not your mind

## Long Hug

I long for a long hug
One without analyzation
One of eternal connection
All regrets washed away
A soft, loving touch
Take me away from this place
This place in my head where I lay in my death bed
Turn the reaper into a sunflower with your smile
There's a safe place in your eyes
I'll keep running as long as I'm with you

## SUNFLOWER

| | | |
|---|---|---|
| Self-Awareness | Seeking | Savage |
| Undeniable | Unvoiced | Unmasked |
| Now | Nostalgia | Nonchalantly |
| Feeling | Following | Fragmentary |
| Loves | Lucrative | Light |
| Orbit | Omens | Originated |
| Waken | Whose | When |
| Existential | Experiences | Escaping |
| Recovery | Resonate | Reality |

## A Mid Life Crisis to Infinity

A mid life crisis
At 20 years old
Blessing or a curse?
BOTH
How to handle spontaneous combustions 101
Cry. Breathe. Listen. Laugh.
LOVE
Every moment is precious
Take it for what it is
Maybe there are no secret codes
Maybe there are no keys
Maybe all the doors are already open
Take a step in
Smell the roses
Taste the fresh air
Touch the light
Feel infinity...

## & Beyond

The codes are secret, until you ask for them
The doors are locked, until you ask for the keys
Ask and you shall receive

Now...do be detailed in these requests
We may send you our best
To find out you wanted less
We hate to hear your mental mess
Yet, we do love putting your strength to the test

Relax, child
The best secrets come to those who are still

## Do Tell

What is it that you THINK I don't understand?
And who the hell are you anyway?

The wiser I become, the less I know....
More interactions are more experiences

Are you telling me you know everything?
Because I'd like to hear it all
Do tell....

## Do Listen

I am NOT sharing my secrets with you
Figure them out yourself

I'll gladly share the fact; you don't know me...
But you'd like to

I amuse you
That smile of yours draws me in
And pulls out my creativity
A match made in heaven; to shine in hell

Change your name from Sensitive Sally to Bodacious Bri
And let's ride

## Tame Me

I wonder if you can tame this crazy mind of mine
Do you like a challenge?
Can we find balance?

Will you be the one to teach me the untold?
Time to watch this movie plot unfold
Before our eyes, hearts and minds

A perfect nightmare
Chase me and I'll chase you

We are one of the few
Who understand this calculated chaos

Followers flock to our kiosk
To buy a piece of what we've got

We'll paint our love in paper thin words
Observe as they try to learn
Why our fire burns so bright

Watch in delight, my love
We've opened doors to the skies above

## Save You

Weave your thoughts into the crevices of my brain
Fill my mind with your chaos
I'll keep you contained in a safe place
One where only lovers go

The touch of your lips; a golden ticket
Let me in your factory
I'll pass all your tests
And clean my mess

## Home Bound

Waking up from a prophetic dream
Longing to be in that moment; anxious

Why can't I have you now?
What am I doing wrong?
What am I doing right?
What will stop the mind spins?

Feeling love deeper than all the words in Webster's

What a simple dream it was
You and I; same place, same time
Humble and patient

Much more to learn before my lips can touch yours
Thinking of making love to you; the only thought leading me
through my darkness

Thank you for loving unconditionally

I'll be home soon

## I've Been Waiting

My dearest Brianna...
Reality is but a dream
A dream is but reality

You are here with me
I am there with you
Two of the same point of view

Love can be made without physical touch
What a magnificent rush
Magic between yours hands
Transformation in your Heart
You've made it to the Land of Love
Step in....
Room has been held for you

## Who You Thought You Knew

You like my energy?
What does it feel like to you?
I feel a mess, well put together
Sweet surface, rough edges
A puzzle whose pieces are lost under the couch
With dust, termites, dead skin and old pens
Old men search my eyes in wonder, in lust
A mystery in the iris of Bri
One you cannot read, for I won't publish it
To myself I stay; lost in my grey haze
You say you feel my light
I contemplate how?
I've shut it off to keep my heart safe...

## Queen

They are drawn to you...
The lost and the confused

You've got what they need
They will feed off your energy

Send you in circles
Then blame you for the consequences of their spirals

It is their puzzle pieces that collect dust, under the thrown you
sit upon
Safely nesting their broken hearts

Take a load off, Mother
Allow the others to rediscover all that was lost

The cost?
Your free will....

## Ego

Yes, I do want to be a part of your journey
No, I do not want to dumb myself down to do so

It seems you are looking down a tunnel Ego created
While I look through it

Ego can be transparent
If you can allow yourself to see

I miss the ignorance of you and I
But, I've grown too much to continue swimming with you

I'm ready to fly, my love
I'll be in the sky

**But, Who Am I?**

How dare you leave me!
I will drown!
How selfish can you be?
Can't you see, you are nothing without me!
Well...I'm nothing without you

So, you're going to leave me here broken apart?
While you are off to a new start!

Disgusting .
Absolutely absurd .
Not one more word
Fly along....

I LIKE MY FISH BOWL

## Balanced Mind

I may never understand and you may never either
That can be beautiful or treacherous;
Depending on the lens we choose

Leave judgment behind and soar;
You majestic creature

## Perception

Perspective sensual lenses
Internal shades
Mother fucking stuntin'
Cause we both chose the same pair
Win-win
Now sip the gin-gin
& stay tinted

# May The Fourth Be With You

I may not be blonde
My hair may not be long
I may not wear thongs
Granny panties cover my cakes
Making up for my raw face
Can you appreciate raw eggs?

Momma bird couldn't imagine me when she got laid
Momma bird couldn't appreciate her raw eggs
Momma bird fights the light with all her might
I pray, one day, momma bird sees the imagination she laid in
her nest of raw eggs

They say beauty is in the eyes of the beholder
So hold my hands
Look into my eyes, into my soul
*Raw* as gold
*Rare* as gold
I'll show you my plans
Let's take a stand
Spread our wings, fly together
Soar over this land
Then lay me down and in our nest shall our raw imagination be
birthed

Inspiration: Songs of Sister Bird by Alexsis Neuman pages 70-71

## Lean On Me

Raw face matches mine
Raw eyes, one of a kind
Nest of twigs intertwined from our rhythm and rhymes
Chirp faint melodies into my ear

I'm addicted to your ambition
Bewildered by your brains
Ceaseless curiosity every time you place your hands on mine
What is our next story line?

We've moved mountains
Dived the deepest of seas
Made it out of the Bermuda Triangle safely

The adventures we take amaze me
Your sparkling smile will forever satisfy my needs

Let's show Momma Bird a love she has never known

## Someone Like Me

I wish I had someone like me
A friend who understands this weirdness
One who motivates me into my creative aura

Our laughter would be constant
Smiles reaching the heavens
The Gods would love watching our stories

Together we'd ripple vibrant colors into the universe
Together we could cry away the pain of others

We would have scavenger hunts
Set up tents of sheets in the living room
Bake cookies for our friends
Write stories to act them out
Experience life then come together to share our perspectives
We'd be inspiration to all who watch our movie

Oh divine, when will it be time?
Bring this friend of mine
Let us shine

## The Blessing Of Family

Sounds like your Sisters are missing from your life
Sounds like your childhood was stripped away
Like the house, when your mother couldn't pay

You ask for a "friend"
You've got three!
Show them the friend in you
How amazing your Love can be!

Famous Florians
Got a ring to it…
Pound that bell!
Break the spell once cast by the Wicked Witch

## Unloved Masterpiece

I juggle my parent's traits

I'd like to think they are everything I hate...
They made me a mold of their love
Shattered clay the day I was birthed
I live to re-piece their masterpiece
Show them the love they lost;
The sum of their love

They had four of us...
Four models of their love
Or un-love, I could say
We felt unloved every day
& to this day the un-love remains the same

## Tin Man

Leaving the problems in the past
Vibrating in the solutions

       I LOVE YOU MOM
       I LOVE YOU DAD

I once reflected the two of you;
Now you reflect me

Everything I am, vibrating in your subconscious
I fought for so long
The war is now over
I am taking our name, putting it in Fame

Tin Man has found the grenade you've stored and used it as a
heart
Sewed your opinions into wings

I fly higher than the rest
I have you to thank for that

## Drowning

Tears crashing down
In this Del Taco booth
Employees send smiles
Teenager hugs me softly
They care. They opened their space to my heart.
Forever grateful
If only my mind could quite down...

## Build A Bridge

Cross over those emotions
Let them flow
As you glow
Above the waters

Send thoughts down the river;
Like the bottle caps you watched race down the gutters

The simple life: when time is only a frame of mind

## Rock Bottom

I believe I've found rock bottom..
The foundation set beneath my feet was never solid
Rocks soggy from words unspoken
Energy being squished out of them the higher I tried to climb
Only to find I may never make it to the top

## Awake

Take it one step at a time
Turn unspoken words into rhymes

Release fears on pages
Release Ego carried for ages

Founding a new pyramid
One big enough for all of Us

Never see the rocky depths of Soul again

## Tug Of War

Tug of war between saving my family or saving myself
How selfish can I be?
Am I selfish, for wanting a different life?
How can I make the transition without loving my roots?
Doesn't seem like I can
My flower isn't growing...
I pray one day after I've rooted and blossomed...
A bee pollinates me with you
We could be a new breed
Oh how lovely that would be
You and me...

## Get To It

Saving yourself is saving your family
You are aware #staywoke
Keep drenching your goals with the watering can of Love
Be an example
Shine your light
& let go of that boy…..
You have business to conduct

## Separated

Who am I without You

Peanuts without butter
Dry

Donkey without Shrek
Lost

Stale cookie dough
Useless

Knowledge without love
Loneliness

I without You
Separated

Your voice in my head
Energy in my bed

Wonder why distance is between us

## Together

You are the sun and I am the moon

You are wind and I am the dust

You are smoke and I am the weed

You are me; I am you

Two as One; One as Two

I love you.

## Toxins

Sweating out my toxins
God, I treat this body like shit
Literally as if it were a sewer for waste
When did I lose my will power?
Where do I build my pyramid of mind, body and soul?
How do I control these programs disguised as instincts?
I know it's a choice
And I allow their choices to influence mine
Whoops…..do I break away or reconnect?

**Try Something New**

Make a choice and stick with it!
Sweets don't taste all that sweet, when you know what they are made of
You choose your battles
You know that….
Will Power is never lost; only strengthened
Their feelings weigh on your shoulders
Put that weight into your hands
Work it like a crystal ball
Control the outcome, Bri Bri

## Where Do I Belong

Living in a world where I do not belong
Mind gone...
One moment at a time
I keep pushing on
These words manifest my destiny
May they rest in me
As I say the things that don't serve me
And swerve what does
What a magnificent rabbit hole
Glory, glory to myself
If I get high, I'm someone else
2, 3 maybe 10 other Bris
Damn it's hard to keep track of me..
This is a catastrophe
Welcome to my rollercoaster
Named enlightenment

### Ride Along

All that shining got you losing your mind?
All that light blinding your sight?
The feeling of the first downward slope;
That is us watching your every move
Doesn't the pressure feel good?
Lose your breath in the moment...
Death and Rebirth
The next hill on your tracks is HIGHER
Good luck preparing for that come down

## Earth Issues

This world is dark
I don't know where to turn; where to start

Oil is polluting our water
And I still fill my gas tank...

$CO_2$ is polluting our air
And I still fill my gas tank...

Pavement is angering Mother Earth
And I still fill my gas tank...

What can I do? Where can I go?
How can I show I know my actions are collectively bringing negativity?

What could I do to change me?
Electric car? Flying car?

Laziness leads me away when I desire to act from my heart

I wrote these words...suppose that's a start...

## It Is What It Is

Put your issues in the tissues and burn them
Set a fire for those desires
Smoke dissipating into parallel universes
Where soul mates await to grant wishes

Your heart is the start
What sets you apart,
From rags to riches

Do what you have to do to make your dreams come true

The Earth is recalibrating
As fear transmutes into love
Give someone a hug
Forget about the pollution

They say "outta sight, outta mind"
We say:
Focus on positives
Trust with all confidence
The universe is shifting
OHANA
No one shall be left behind

## Humble

If I'm humble, could I keep YouTube?
Could I be a face of change?
Am I stealing someone's light...
Someone's soul?
I am scared of the Truth
It haunts me
The monster in my closet
Chasing me through my dreams
To turn and face the Truth could shatter the existence I've
created
Could I put the broken pieces back together?

## Bumble B

Girlllll, yes!
Do you, boo boo
You are the *voice* of change; the face is a perk
Two choices; Love or Fear
Choose wisely….

## Leave My Ego Alone

Telling me I'm beautiful only strokes Ego

Stroke my Soul
See the darkness underneath my light
See the pain in my eyes
Feel the grief of my universe

Understand the beauty beyond this body

That's a true compliment

### It's My Ego Too

I say you are beautiful BECAUSE I see your darkness
I stroke Ego, because Ego separates us
I believe we are separated to learn
Otherwise, we'd all be Adam....

## Color My Dictionary

Language is power
Words burn blue
Desires orange
I may get a lot more than what I thought I asked for
Everything I see playing tricks on me
Flight or fight...
Make peace with perception

Working for a space of my own
A place to call home
I can scream, laugh..poo my pants
No one around stomping my ground

Putting these words together in an uncharted zone
Not alone...
Cramped space
Where is my place?
I know who I can be
If only I'd let me be free

Ideas, ideas, ideas
Sprinkling in my head
Oh the dread of too many
More than can ever be done...
It's the circle, the circle of my life


Careful what you ask for Bri...

# Dun Dun Dun

Ask and you shall receive….
One Golden platter coming your way!
Do not over eat, young one
The food pyramid alone will not fill your belly

Fill your soul
With vibrations of new and old
There is bliss in the silence
There is love in stillness
There are answers when all is forgotten

Must I remind you?
The days of old are upon us
Less is more

Trek on
Head high

The door will be open
When you return Home

## Mistakes

One mistake
Two mistakes
Three mistakes
Four
A few more as I run to the door
Door of *self destruction*: ENTER
Leave behind my fears, clearly not needed here
Pull the lever Kronk!
Send me into the grey maze
Subconscious working in a mysteries ways
I can't make it out alive...
I'll paint the walls while I'm inside

## Lessons

One lesson
Two lessons
Three lessons
Four
Turn the fuck around!
Stay away from that door!
Know there is no lock once you've entered
They are coming for you Bri Bri

Welcome to the Jungle

. . . .

# Part 2:
# The Depths

Here you will read poems that stand alone. I followed the feels to the midst of the ocean. Only to the middle...the deeper emotions within me will be reflected in the sequel, Truce.

I have come to love this midpoint. It is a place where I feel peace and clarity. I find myself lost in this area. Not all who are lost wish to be found.....

xoxox

## SPACE

Space in place...
Lol kidding, who rhymes anyway?

You are in MySpace
Do you come with coding?
Does it fit in my About Me section?
Can I add you to my top 10?
How about space 1?

Wait...that space is filled by    me
Space 2 by                        myself
Space 3 by                        I

You could be my number 4
As long as you don't ask for more;
Than what I am already giving

Test your luck in *my*space
*Bri's* place

I'll devour your...face
Hahaha kidding, I don't like my meat roasted

## Head Phones

I've been listening to your thoughts….the ones you think no one can hear while you've got me shoved in your ears. That guy you've been thinking about, the one you dream of marrying; he thinks about you too, but he only wants to fuck…

Now now, do not be crushed by Truth. I've been listening to other things too. Your heart beat plays faint melodies through my wires. The vibration transforming me into Human; moment and moment again.

I've also been listening to your vocals. Sing in the shower babe. Leave me in the bedroom.

Xoxox

# Kleenex

Take the makeup off
Clear the unnecessary atoms from your eyes
I know you feel death inside
Can you let it go?
Can you rise from the ashes before they float away in the wind?

Mend broken thoughts
Fill cracks with laughter
Keep an eye on the ones who smile; they will lead you home

As roles reverse, you may find yourself handing out the Kleenex
instead of receiving them
Comfort the darkness you once felt
Shed light through understanding and empathy

Use the Kleenex to wipe away literacy
Find metaphors; be free

## Programs

Can one learn to Love?
I am having quite a hard time doing so

I could easily play the victim
Poor Brianna, her childhood was lost

If it had been any different
I may not be where I am NOW

I was prepped for greatness
Just keep swimming, swimming, swimming

Sadness. Happiness.
The emotions I *know*

That is a fair balance
Wouldn't you agree?

Both  s i m u l t a n e o u s l y  hit
CRAZY BRI BACK AGAIN
DID YOU MISS HER?

## Keep An Eye

Patterns mold into mud
Newborns hatched in the abyss
To grow in "shape"

Calculated chaos

Prayer. Save me once, save me twice.
Save me a thousand times
A thousand eyes watching
A thousand eyes waiting
Two thousand hands handling strings

Don't dare break the mold
They're waiting to swarm
To eat you from the inside out
Leave you upside down
No perception of right or wrong

No forgiveness for the wicked
Not that they would ask for it…..

## Whose Call Is It Anyway

I've become a slave to my mind
Worst part; I've grown accustom to this life style
I could say it is comforting, but I would be lying

I am no different from the dictators
The pastors and preachers
The presidents
The occultists

We are idealists.
Our ideas – our way

I justify thoughts
Reaffirm "good intentions"
Deeeeep down, I *crave* thought
I lust for the voices
As soon as they're silenced, I run back for more

"I want to give children a safe place to educate themselves"

Who THE FUCK do I think I am?
What makes my idea more efficient than theirs?
Where does this path lead?
When does the haze clear?
Why do the voices need justification?
How do I return to Him?

# I AM

I am Bri

Bri lives a life style that comes with large sacrifices

Sacrificing ideas of world peace
A fantasy once held
One that quickly faded behind dollar bills

Bri's beast feeds off darkness
He chews on stones thrown
He slurps insecurities
He swallows being's deepest desires

Beasts name is Empathy
Egos name is Sympathy
They are the Trilogy

Bri feels no need to take on your shit
Beast's food bowl is the toilet
Careful passing through the hall...
Ego waits holding the key to the bathroom door

" What is your issue?" Ego asks
Disguised curiosity
Your problems twist new ideas into his mind
New rhymes that will bring a fortune in time

All these emotions laid out before Bri; for her picking
Wild like the flowers in her garden
Some she will allow growth
Others are plucked...

# Introvert

Otherwise known as *internal chaos*
Cannot seem to pull this mask off
Hidden affairs in the air
Secrets spewing from a sleeping mind

Halfway aware of the scars I carry
Beginning to see patterns
Grasping to what I know
Not willing to let ghosts go

Anxiety sweeps over when I consider a new path
What would come if I dared?
I refuse to step into the unknown
Maybe it is written that I stay forever alone

This is a perception of mind
A collective energy
I couldn't be the only one feeling this way
Rise against the demons...

Or do I let their cries fill my lungs?
Drown in their tears
Runaway with their fear
      Oh dear.

I am smart enough to know I do not handle these emotions alone
I must be who I am meant to be
Cast your stones to my thrown

## Nor

Your words cut into my Soul or is that my Ego…?

Learning or analyzing?

Observant or sensitive?

Must I choose between the two?

They say "you're human"
I see that as no excuse

Heaven on Earth
Whatever Heaven is to you

I find myself lost in theologies, pastries and *your* eyes

I lost that rhyme but it was not time
Our stars *still* have yet to align

Must be this crazy mind of mine

Am I crazy?
Or does everyone lie?
To make it through a world locked in time

Fuck this time and fuck your lies
See you on the Other Side

## Easy Way Out

I see the easiest way...
To what?
To suppress my Darkness
Which is?
Leaning on another being's happiness
How so?
Giving them what they want in exchange for what I want
What do they want?
Someone to grow with
What do you want?
Someone to lean on
What is wrong with that?
That is what we *WANT*
What we need...well...
We *NEED* to love ourselves
We are weakened by desires
We are strengthened by Spirit
Spirit thrives when desires are set aside
I desire his affection and attention
The wise say: if you love someone, let them go
Goodbye, fantasies
Good riddance....
Here and Now; I AM COMPLETE
The Darkness can no longer haunt me
I am Free

## WHY

God, damn me. Why couldn't I be who I you needed when our eyes met? I *knew* it was not time to see you. I knew I was not ready for what was to come.

But you kept calling. Praying to see me. Begging to know I was real. Bet you could have never imagined the pain I was going to put you through.

That is my perception. Never confirmed by you. Not out loud, at least. I'd like to think I hear you in my head.

Four. Four times I can say without a doubt it *was* you. Asking "why?" What a solid question. You found me, then sent me back for the answer.

Now you sweep my mind at any given moment. I am left with the whys.

Why did you refuse to let me live without knowing you?
Why did you sit quietly as I struggled?
Why did you let me leave?
Why couldn't you save me?

I hope your *why* was answered…..
Mine still hurt; make me shake and cry, because, I DON'T KNOW WHY!

I don't know why I'm still here and you're there; on the other side. I can't find why my feet won't move in your direction. I won't ask how to return.

I reach for the projection of you. My heart cries. My mind does not have the capacity to circulate the *whys*.

I do know that I love you, and I do not know how you could forgive me for what I've put you through.

## Devotion

What a long year it's been
And through the Darkness you stayed...
I am amazed
My mind hazed with confusion
Eyes glazed from isolation
One graze of your hands against my skin and I'm ready to settle

I've been a wild goose
All jungle cats hunting my trail
One after another, I failed
A cold spell over my heart
While we were far apart

Never far in heart
As you patiently awaited my return
Took burn after burn
Each time I turned and walked away

I led myself into a grey maze with no ending; no RIGHT turns
Today I've grown wings
Tonight I fly into the sky
Ready to lay in the clouds with you
My dearest...

Thank you for waiting
You are amazing
I am learning to love...
You and myself as One

## Meet Again

I never hid from the light
Only dimmed mine
To keep safe from the views of others
That shouted in the back of my mind

Feelings I felt; they were never mine
An Angel of Empathy
Guided by time

Our paths crossed, our stars aligned
But yours shined brighter than mine

You're three steps ahead
I feel far behind
"Hello" and "Goodbye" simply to shelter the Ego of mine
I will learn to love again; all in due time

Tell me the spot where we'll meet
Show me the scars on your feet
The ones you got walking across hot rocks for me

Inspired by Mikaela Gordan's piece Nothing Like You

## Ode To Spiders

Bushes trimmed
Life lost
Where do the spiders go?

Ever think about the privileges of life?
You think you own your home….
At any given time it could be taken away
A fire
The government
The irs
A flood
A war
What would you do if it crumbled before you?
How upset would you be letting a higher power determine your
fate?

Imagine being a spider creating life in the bushes of the park
Imagine living every day in the same web

Now imagine a landscaper trimming away your home….
He can't hear your screams
He can't feel your pain
He has a job to do….

Physical reality is a privilege

You may be forced to adapt to changes
How will you respond?

Where is your soul?
Is it with your physical reality?
Can you move beyond?
Can you adapt?

Would losing it all result in your lose of self?
Who are you?
What do you stand for?
What keeps your spirit alive?

What power determines fate?
You, Us, Them, Him
Simultaneous moments combusting
Every action with reactions; ripples in the web
What is the center of YOUR universe?
Family, job, creativity...
Pick one, watch the web it weaves

From this perspective, can you understand the scared trees?
Life lies in the eyes of those living
Take a second look
Before you cast hooks

## It Was Always Us But Never We

To all of you who could never see
The love that was deep within me...
Congratulations, you lucked out
A storm was brewing in my heart
Awaiting another's love who I would tear apart

To you, who I have torn apart
I am giving back the pieces of your heart
You were gold while I was bronze
Your light shined while mine dimly flickered on and off
I stole your torch and only let you shine on my time
And for that, my deepest condolences
It was always Us, but never We
And now I see that we could not be two lights in the same torch
So I will shine on my porch,
For the next who knocks at my door

To you, brave enough to step onto my porch, kudos.
I admire you.
But does my light distract you from your path?
Or do you wish to feel the wrath of darkness that lies behind the
door before you?
A key, please? You ask, sincerely
You crave my lust, so I will send you on a hunt
I'll summon my demons to test your luck
Will you make it through the maze to the magic formula that
opens the deepest part of me?
Let's say you do...

You've conquered the opportunity to turn Us into We
What will you choose, oh courageous one?
Row, row, row your boat down my deep blue sea
Now you've got a taste of what we aren't meant to be
I thank you for your presence
My light now shines brighter than before
I raise my hand and point to the door
You hate to leave but I love to watch you walk away
I return to my rooftop, my vision magnified by a telescope
Searching for a kindred spirit in the sky


To you, my angel
I see you in the clouds above my home
I wish you would come back down
You wish I would rise up
But it seems I am stuck
In the prison funded by lack of imagination
These walls a figment of my creations
I had set my mind on you and attempted to follow your path
Little did I know, with each leap you took, you never looked back
The marks you left faded to black
And now I wander the darkness of what we "could" be
While you silently watch me
You project images of We
If only I could let go
Set myself apart from the walls I built as art
Grow wings and soar above
Could you wait on that cloud, my love?
I know this is a selfish request

Your heart being put to the test
How long must you wait until We can be put to rest?
If only I had the answers to the scantron of our love...


Inspired by Mikaela Gordan's poem *I Love Vous: On Polyamory*

## Soul Sister

I may not be perfect

I don't make it every time you need me
I don't always answer the phone
I forget to respond to messages
I didn't buy you a birthday card

What do all those have in common?
They're mundane….

We are deeper than that
Our souls connect with a thick silver cord
We share feelings, experiences, and thoughts
We have the ability to understand the other

But you're upset…
You're always upset if it isn't your way

I have a way too…
I have feelings too…
I have dreams too…

Tell me why you choose this negative mindset
I know you better than that

You're a shining star
You are an artist
You are a go getter

When did the universe lose you?

Please don't let your light burn out
We will ALL suffer
We need you
I need you

I've always needed you...

It wasn't fair the separation we faced as children
We needed each other
We were best friends
How could they tear us apart?

Adults never seem to understand

Without me, you stopped eating
Without you, I terrorized the neighborhood

We were good together

Peanut butter and jelly
Chocolate and marshmallows
A printer with ink
A canvas with art

Yet they tore us apart

And here we are...

Adults. Able to choose ourselves
Decide our destines
Clearly communicate our hearts

But I cannot...
I cannot open up to you
I cannot speak my Truth

God damn it, they've ruined you

My best friend
My soul sister
Lost in a cloud of negative emotions
Bowing down to kiss your feet isn't enough

Know this...I will always be here
In heart and in Spirit

The day we reconnect the angels will rejoice!
Again you will have your voice
Oh how I miss that sound...

## Scooby Doo

Oh doo doo breath
How I miss your morning kisses
Your paws planted on my pillow
Eyes brighter than the full moon

This year has been ruff ruff without you

Forgive me Scooby Doo
For abandoning you
Packing my belongings without explanation
Closing the door behind my suit cases

I grabbed everything...except for you

Oh doo doo, my doo doo

I joke it off; the same way my father did
Tell me Scooby, do dogs feel sorrow too

No need to answer
I see it in your eyes each time I close the door
You scream for more time

Is time even relevant to you?

I feel you Scooby. I know you feel me too
No matter the distance, your frequency is one I can connect to

I feel your boredom Scooby Doo
We always had something to do when I took care of you

Now you sit at home
Hit after hit, he takes another bong rip
All his attention faced at the tv screen
He doesn't hear your screams for attention
He doesn't notice you are gaining weight
He could never connect to you like I can
Can we blame him?
Our childhoods are quiet similar Scooby Doo
They say history repeats itself...
I say, fuck history!

I can change our worlds Scoody Doo
Turn 1 into 2
We'll leave 3 an 4 at the door

We will rewrite our scripts
Shake our hips, as we explore every nook

We will make the most of each moment
Travel far and wide
Meet souls of all kinds

Don't tell him where we've been
He doesn't understand why we do what we do
He cannot feel what we feel

The chronicles of BriBriFresh and Scooby Doo

## Ten Of Me

Wait……..wait. STOP
NOOOOOO
Bad idea
Realllllll bad idea
Real realllllll bad idea!

**OK! O FUCKING K! I won't do it…again**

Yeah? Doubt it. You monster.
Now, go on
Make a YouTube video

**Nooooooo schedule a photo shoot!**
**We want photos! We want photos!**
**n.a.k.e.d. photos**
**#sendnudes**

Shut up. I am tired of *tracking* "likes"
Stay home. Alone. Hibernate.
Pretend you are sleeping if anyone knocks

**Y'all trippin.**
**It is time to shake what ya momma gave ya**
**Use that voice too**

Now now now
That is no way to evolve
Go to the forest and pray

**Pray? HA! Pray some In-n-Out into existence**
**A Tootsie Pop and cigar for dessert**

None of that sounds as appealing as reading a book or two or
five

**IDEA! Call a friend, go out, black out, yolo**

GOOD FUCKING NIGHT
*wake me up when I'm wiser and I'm older*

## Dirty Woman

What am I but a pigment of my own imagination?
What am I but what you observe me to be?

I am a dirty woman
The one who brushers her teeth without toothpaste
The one who extends no shave November into May
The one who wears the same outfit 3 days in a row
The one who refuses to use shampoo or body wash
The one whose mustache grows thicker than Sasquatches
The one who wears 2 year old thongs; the stench undeniable
The one who lives in a car

How dare I park in your 24 hour fitness parking lot
How dare I sleep naked because the morning Vegas heat
beating through my car windows is unbearable
How dare I take the easy way out
How dare I sleep in a car when you work your ass off for that
house
How dare I live "free" when you are shackled by your lack of
imagination
How dare I be proud of myself

Proud to face my demons
Proud to carry a confidence you never allowed me to have
Proud to say I am BriBriFresh

Fresh perspective following each moment in the time line I call
life
Fresh out of jail after telling BLM to fuck off
Fresh skid marks on your driveway to remind you of the day I
left
The day I stood up for my dirty soul

Thank you for all the grenades you watched blow me to pieces
Thank you for all the wooden spoons you broke spanking my ass
Thank you for every slap in the face
Thank you for telling me I would never amount to anything

You fueled my fire
You challenged me to prove myself
You gave me 1 million reasons to never give up
You created a monster
Numb to feelings
Without emotion I trek on
No money could buy the mask I've created

In the end...you were always right
I am nothing
I see death in my eyes
I see the shadows that consume my mind
I see a fish gasping for breath

I see 4 year old Brianna crying behind the couch when pops left
I see 7 year old Brianna screaming, sobbing banging on your
locked bedroom door
I see 14 year old Brianna leaving the OBGYN with a prescription
for birth control yet no understanding of sexual intercourse
I see 17 year old Brianna leaving a wrecked home
I see 22 year old Brianna frantically trying to escape a past
darker than the back side of the moon
I see the hugs that I never received
I see the kisses I never felt
I see the secrets I still hide from you

The secrets I hide from everyone
Because I am a dirty woman

The filth has stained my soul
The words have punctured every inch of my being
I believe every nasty opinion you throw as if I am robbing you of
your identity

I am what you observe me to be
I am my hazed imagination

## Childhood Story

My head cannot understand our distance
Ego spins me into insanity
Live to save Brianna from emotional distress
The child inside running from emotion
Hiding from the Truth
Crying in a closet

Although everyone can hear; no one comes to aid
No one else could take on this suffering
No one else would understand

Born empathic without understanding of emotions
Feeling mom's pain
Avoiding mom's pain
Physically pained from mom; not understanding her pain

Feeling dad's restlessness
Need to be outside
Cannot. Single mother can't keep track of me out there.
Stay inside Brianna. Be quiet.

Feeling grandma's OCD after years of programming
You're a Virgo, you're organized
I'd say compulsive; I'd say struggling

Feeling my baby sisters' need for a father
I can step up. Brianna in charge.
Mom doesn't like that

Though mom is never home; working to support us
When she is, she sleeps
When she wakes, I am shunned for stepping up

Brianna thinks she knows everything...
I WAS connected to Spirit, to Source
I WAS creative and cunning
I DID protect her family

Years of being shamed lead me into extreme darkness
Silver lining in the far distance
No love inside myself
Where can I find this love!?

I searched high and low
I searched every soul in school
Hoping to find the love I lost

Nothing came close. No one understood me.
One friend at a time. That was all I could handle.
When the friend was gone I could not face myself
I couldn't face my mom, sisters or dad

I settled.
Settled for everything I wasn't
Settled for pain; lost the love
Settled for physical; spiritual death
I traded my dirty mirror for his
Watched my mirror decay in his arms
As I tried and tried to polish his

Put his mirror on a pedestal
He buried mine six feet under
If I am going down...you are coming down with me

A gun in the bed side dresser
Threats of death
Sobs so heavy my body sank in the carpet

Meanwhile my family was happy for me
Praised my success

Brianna will be a lawyer
Brianna bought a home, she's only twenty
Brianna how much longer must we wait for your wedding

My family knew I was wearing a mask

His family heard the sobs; suggested medication
So deep in their own darkness
They couldn't properly face ours
And I couldn't face theirs; avoid, avoid, avoid

Alone in the quiet, Spirit whispered the truth
My heart longed to let go
My ego wasn't ready to be destroyed
I had two choices...
Leave or kill this body

I left. Left everything.

The boy, the house, the dogs, the job, the money, the
belongings, the emotions
I was numb
I was scared
Worst of all, I was shunned
The owners of glass houses threw theirs stones
Chucked them as if I was a river for hopping rocks

Brianna how could you do that?
What will you do now?
You'd better get a job
What's your plan?
Brianna I knew you wouldn't last, you should have listened

Years of bottled emotions
With no one to share with
No one would listen without judgment
Alone
Desperate

There must be another male out there willing to take me;
willing to understand

Avoided my mom, sisters and dad
I couldn't go back to them...
I couldn't let them hurt me again...

Without guidance, I asked acid
Who am I?

I found myself in Long Beach, on a pier
No parking, no gas, food or friends
Defeated
Break down

Snapchat will listen
People saw
No one asked
Brianna is crazy; I'll stay away from her

Back to Nevada; leave emotions behind
Need. Love.
Back to my ex.
Back to my darkness

A music festival; Lightening in a Bottle
How I felt...may as well go
Ego pulling my hair "don't go"
Stay home, stay secure in what you know

Spirit whispered it'd be worth it

He stood in front of me
A smile I'll never forget

He's gorgeous; I'm shy
I'm sweating, I'm annoyed
Distracted, overwhelmed, irritated, thirsty

We're wearing the same hat...

I never wear hats
Fist bump to that
Back to my head

I hurt him; I felt it
Why do I feel it?
How do I know what he's feeling without asking?
What's he doing in my head?
We'd only spoken seven words

I don't understand this
I don't like not understanding...

I don't ask. Can't.
I couldn't put it into words
Ego refused to let me
Ego refused the idea of letting walls down
Brianna you've been hurt too many times; don't let a handsome
face fool you
And that is where a new chapter began…..

## Hallelujah

Truth be told, they are still on my mind; the men I thought I left behind
There is a battle within that I am tired of fighting
This seems to be a game of love
A game I cannot win

All along, you've been here
You see, I've got issues but you've got them too
So give yours to me and I'll give mine to you

I think back to the day I wrote you into existence
You are everything I asked for
I wasn't ready
Truthfully, I've never been ready for anything I asked for

Time has made me stronger
I can give more love than ever before
Yet, I feel selfish

Selfish for making you wait
Selfish for expecting you to want me now
Selfish because I still wonder about the men I never had

Addicted to the chase
As if there is a trophy at the end
As if there is an *end*
As if love is *only* a game

Love is life
Love is learning
Love is growth

I want to grow with you
I hope you can forgive me
I am still going to think about them...the other men
I love them
I love what they taught me
I love their reflections
But, I could never paint myself in their portraits
I would change to fit in their dreams
I've stopped
What is my dream?
I'll tell you...

I see myself in a house full of art
I'll cook delicious meals
Keep everything clean cause OCD be one tidy mother fucker!
I can be creative and goofy
Sing at the top of my lungs
Bang on drums
Watch movies and pause when I want to analyze scenes
Read books
WRITE
Make videos and record podcasts
LAUGH
Grow food and pretty flowers
Use natural products
MEDITATE

LOVE GOD

I see my home as one all are welcome to
A place people love to be at because the vibes are magnificent
An open door with UNDERSTANDING on the front matt
Music of all kinds
Creative arts
Clear communication
Open hearts
Alignment
Happiness
Family
Freedom
Service
Gratitude

I see me and you
I have a lot of work to do
Doing it alone has me distracted
I've made choices I am not proud of
My physical being is not in the best health
My mentality is chaos
My emotions run wild
My spirit awaits my return...

I am tired of burning and rebuilding
I want to settle and build a foundation
I want to see you each morning
I want to wear a glow from our love
I want to tell others we are together

I want us to trust
I want us to build bridges
I want to rid of need for attention for the wrong reasons
I want to focus; on me, on you, on us and on what we can give
back to the world

I am scared
Scared of failure
Mostly scared of success
This could be a wild ride
Are you ready?

## TO BE FREE... (POETIC DIALOGUE)

Posted on August 13, 2017 by Mikavelli (MG)
mikaelagordan.com

How free can we be
When free is different to you and me

*To be free of sickness and pain
or to be free from knowledge that constrains?*

Knowledge is freedom
Sickness constrains

*Pain strengthens
Love liberates*

In freedom we find power
In power, freedom diminishes

*Humbled and meek
Freedom we seek
To love is to be free...*

To love is to feel pain
Can freedom be found in both, simultaneously?

*To forget pain, to embrace change
Can surrendering to love be the key?*

What if the door was never locked
And surrender was not the answer

*What if love wasn't a battlefield*
*And freedom didn't mean war?*

Freedom meant contentment
Contentment meant no lessons learned

*Our lessons were our blessings*
*Freedom means progressing*

Progressing to larger mountains
A new climb in time

*Atop the Peak, see the world from afar*
*Enchanted by city lights*

City lights bring me fright when viewed from above
They flicker like freedom, on and off.

*To reemerge in the city*
*To be one with the light — to be free.*

The lights are cut; now only the moonshine can guide

*In the dark we hide*
*The secrets in us they confide*

Open confinement when darkness comes about
One in the same when light could not display differences

*Echoes in the distance, silence surrounds*
*Unity and harmony, love and deliverance.*

Peace of mind
True freedom found

*Serenity of the heart*
*Tranquility resounds*

Beats of infinity
Rhythms of entity.

*MG* and BB

*This poem itself is collaboration with M. Gordan, inspired through conversations and poetry. The sharing of thoughts and connectivity of ideas bloomed with collaboration.*
*#InternationalPoetry*

## The Art Of Reappearing

Why be a leaf when you can be a branch of leaves?
Why stop there when you can be the entire tree?

Why keep your leaves to yourself?
Why not allow them to roam freely with no destination but
astoundment at landing?

Why hide from the world you see?
Is it not *but* a projection of your inner wounds and inner peace?

My dear, do not hide from thy.
Thy will find a way into your life.

Do not run from thy.
Thy has angels waiting at every pit stop.

Thy love you and ask for love in return.
Is that too sensitive for your wounded heart?


Inspired by The Art of Disappearing by Naomi Shihab Nye

### Engagement

Engagement engagement engagement
Between you and I
A thought ring ring ringing in my head
Of a ring on this finger of mine
Why does a ring of some sort represent engagement?
When engagement could be the conversation between you and
I
A not so scared act that seems scarce in this society
When engagement may only appear if you are willing to engage
Not just elope; but engagement in physical intercourse
Engagement bringing both our demons to light
Engagement moaning in delight
Engagement can bring a fright
When engagement was lacking in the childhood of mine
Now engagement only comes time to time with a price to pay
for its rhythm and rhyme

## Lighthouse

We were both taught to suck it up
To take their shit
Hear their opinions
Feel their pain

We were both taught to keep our mouths shut
To jump when told
To shut up
To sit up

What is the difference between us?
You have let the silence be engrained into your soul
I refuse the silence
I have a voice to be used
I have an opinion to be shared
I have love far deeper than the scars they left

I feel sorrow for you
Knowing you were once a lighthouse for those lost in their
emotions
Knowing you still are, occasionally
You are in heart
Now you silently scream to those you see lost, but they cannot
hear you
If only they could see you...

# DNA

I get it
Finally

We live vicariously through DNA
Through the mix of our ancestors
Through the mixing of their juices

I wondered why I was lead to you
I wondered why I held you so high
I wondered why you never fit my expectations

What was meant as a reminder of Self
Turned into lose of Self
Shoving dreams down the other's throat

We share DNA
Our paths meant to cross at one moment
Then separate and move upward for the rest

Again we will meet
A moment in time
Is all it is meant to be

Monogamy is crazy to me
To be with one
Even in the moments our DNA is unstrung

How could I expect one to keep it together?

When DNA refuses to merge as One
Forever two strands in the same direction

That is us
That is every relationship I see
Two climbing the same tree
See you at the top, my friend

## Hope

I despise everything that makes me think of you, except for you
I despise every word I read that reminds me of you, except the
words you write
I despise every face I see that resembles you, except for yours

I despise it all because I despise myself
Despise the way I turned around
Despise that I could not leave my mind in time to kiss you
Despise longing for your electric touch
Despise knowing where you are and that place is out of reach
Despise that you will not come for me
Despise the sentence I've placed upon myself

Yet, I could never despise you
There is Hope in my Heart
Faith that I will see you again
And in that moment, we will embrace
An embrace we have waited patiently for
One that will stop our worlds
It will shake others
We will create a new existence within our hearts

At least, this is my Hope

# Part 3:
# Dale Florian

These next few poems were written by my father, Dale Florian. They are about a decade old. It seems as if I am picking up where he left off and he was picking up where my grandfather left off.

POPS, thank you for supporting me. You help keep me afloat when I begin to drown in emotions. You have taught me to see life from multiple perspectives. You are not always the rock under my feet, but you are the owl, watching my moves and swooping in when asked. I appreciate you for reminding me of your love. I am thankful for your kind words. I am glad to call you my dad.

(Mom, I love and appreciate you. Without you, I am nothing. If you had poems, they would be in here too)

# LOVE AT FIRST SIGHT

On the flat face of an object
With a glow, oh so bright
Letters join, words connect ...
People talk when they write.

Rythmless tapping, it's almost morning
As I kept staring into the light
Life's dream was unwrapping, surprise, then, forming...
The mail arrived late last night

Opening it, as I yawned, to see from whom it would be
Unaware and unprepared of the torch she would lite
My heart stopped. It even skipped a beat. ..
It was Love At First Sight

Still in awe, now, this next morning
Tho shit still don't feel quite right
Since reality stepped in to remind me. . .
My dream girl and I may, still, never unite

So in this bottle, I insert this note .
Sealed with a kiss and put the lid on tight.
I reach waaay back n give it a throw. .
And pray it gets to her alright

I'm dreaming of the day she gets it
And out loud she starts to recite
The title in which I gave to it ...
I called it, "Love At First Sight"

It read: I thanked the Lord Jesus
With all His Power and Might

For fulfilling my dreams & prayers...
With a Love At First Sight

But for if some strange reason
The Lord decides to overwrite
And doesn't find it pleasing. . .
For you & I to unite

You'll always remain in my thoughts .
With your picture locked away tight
For in those days of loneliness. . .
Looking at you will make my sun shine bright

I always knew there was a heaven
And now I know dreams come true
Cuz from the very first moment _ _ _ _
I FELL IN LOVE WITH YOU

THANK YOU ALL
Your Friend
Dale Florian

# MEDITATION

What's Up Y'all? Just Felt Like Passing On Some Of Lifes
Teachings, Lessons, And Blessings That Most Of Just Don't See;
Mainly Cuz Of Greed, Or Selfishness, Or Just Too Blind And
Shallow. Ya-Know... With All The Pollution In The World, And,
Poverty, And, The Outrageous Number Of Teen Suicides... Why
Aren't We More Thankful And Realize How Well Off And Lucky
We ALL Really Are. No Matter How Old, Or Rich, Or Intelligent
We Can We Could Always Learn More And Improve Ourselves
And Help Pass It On To Improve The World Around Us. We Need
To Remember That, Sometimes Not getting What We Want
Could Be A Real Stroke Of Luck. When We Realize We've Made
A Mistake, We Need To Take Immediate Steps To Correct It. We
All NeEd To Have Respect, Foremost, For Ourselves, Respect For
Others, And Take Responsibility For Our Actions. When We
Lose, We Must Not Lose The Lesson. We Should Always Open
Ourselves To Change, But Not Let Go Of Our Values. We Need
To Share Our Knowledge... It's A Good Way To Achieve
Immortality. We Should Always Judge Our Success By What We
Had To Give Up In Order To Get It. We Should Live A Good,
Honorable Life. Cuz Then, When We Grow Older, We Can Think
Back And Enjoy It A Second Time. If We Took Into Account That
Great Love And Great Achievements Take Great Risks, We'd
Probably Feel More Rewarded, Or Strive Harder. We Can't Ever
Let A little Dispute Injure A Great Friendship. A Loving
Atmosphere In Our Home Is Yet The Strongest Foundation For
Our Life. In Disagreements With Our Lovedones, We Need Only
To Deal With The Current Situations And Not Bring Up The Past.
And... The Best Relationship Is The One In Which Our Love For
Our Other Exceeds The Need For The Other. And Silence Is
Sometimes The Best Answer. And Mainly... We Need To Spend
Time Alone, Everyday, And Take A Deep Breath, And Close Our
Eyes, Think About Lifes "GOODS" And What We DO Have. Feel

That Tingle Inside? And Everyday, Look Far, And Realize ... On That Final Day Of Truth ... Don't We All Want The Prize!?

I Wish Us All A Good Life!

Dale Florian

## LISA

Lisa Loved Horseback Riding,
Her Friends, And Parties Too.
But When It Came To Painting,
That's All She Wanted To Do.
She Painted Everything She Saw,
Birds, Flowers... Even The Sky
Some Days She Sat In Her Window
And Painted Everything That Passed By
But Lately She'd Been Feeling Woozy
And Her Muscles Ached A lot
And Her Parents Got Kinda Worried
So They Took Her To The Doc
The Dr. Took Some Tests
To Make Sure Everything Was OK
Then The Nurse Came Out With A Sad Look
And Here's What She Had To Say...
I'm Sorry But You Have Leukemia
And Maybe, Just 3 Months More
Lisa Jumped Up And Ran Out The Room
And Slammed The Office Door
She Ran Down The Street Screaming
She Cried Her Eyes Out Till They Were Dry
Stayed Wide Awake The Entire Night
Wondering What It's Like To Die
Her Parents Hugged Her Tightly
Saying, "We Love You Very Much,
We'll Be With Eachother Forever,
You Know We'll Always Be In Touch
So They All Moved Down To Florida,
Where Lisa Wanted To Spend Her Last Days
Painting Everything She Could...
And Horseback Riding By The Bay

She Woke Up One Morn And The Weather Was Bad
She Was Depressed Having To Sit Inside All Day
So Her Mom Took Her Shopping...
Thats Where She met Jay. They Spent A lot Of Time Together
Collecting Seashells And Always Talking
The Best 4 Weeks Of Her Life Went By
Then, One Day When They Were Walking
With Words Carved That Read, "I Love You"
Jay Handed Her A Ring
Lisa Smiled As Big As Ever
And Her Heart Began To Sing
The Very Next Moment, She Shed A Tear
Then Out Rolled # 2
She Explained About Her Leukemia
"That Doesn't Matter!" Said Jay, "I Love You!"
So Everyday They Spent Together
Doing Whatever They May
Lisa's Heart Was Getting Weaker
She Found It Hard To Stay Awake
She, Then, Painted Her Finest Picture
And She Gave It To Jay
She Said, "For You To Always Remember Me By"
When I Have To Leave This Place
They Then Left For A Walk
Searching For Sea Shells . Lisa Collapsed, And Was Losing Her
Breath
And Said, "Jay Please Hold My Hand"
"I Love You More Than Anyone...
You Are My Only True Love!
But Now My Time Is Up...
I'll Watch Over You From Above"
All-The-Sudden, Lisa's Body Was Lifeless
As She Lay In Jays Arms
He Sat There The Rest Of The Day...

And He Kept Her Safe From Harm!

So Please, Friends...
Let Someone Know You Love Them
Cuz We Don't Know What Tomorrow Holds
And EVERYBODY Wants Love
And To Those People Who Don't Have All That Much...
LOVE Means Everything To Them... Its All That Matters!!!
And If You've Ever Faced Death Before...
Thats All You Think About ...
Is Who You Didn't Say "Bye" To
And Tell Them "I LOVE YOU!"
Trust Me On That...


Dale Florian

## Acknowledgements:

HUGE thank you to my youngest sister, Gia Florian, for allowing me to use her art work!! The cover was her vision a few years back. I remember the day I saw it hanging on her wall, I was mesmerized. I love you Gia! Your strength inspires me. Seeing passion in your eyes keeps me out of the darkest places. You are an amazing being with a bright future ahead.

Thanks go to Alexsis Neuman for her book Songs of Sister Bird! Her writing and her light inspired me to publish my words. You can buy her book on Amazon, Kindle and CreateSpace. You can follow her on Instagram @valiantmermaidpoetry.

Thank you to MG, Mikaela Gordan. I found you on Instagram as @mg.poetree and immediately felt the need to know you. From there I found your blog. Your ways with perceptions could sway any being into creative writing. You can read the marvelous work on mikaelagordan.com.

Thanks Gma Florian. I will always reminisce on our phone call when I told you I was putting a book together and you told me, "Brianna, this is a day to remember. This is the day you have begun your life. I am marking this in my journal." When you are proud of me, I feel like I can fly.

AND THANK YOU to all who had sparked interested when I shared my thoughts. All of you kept my North Star shining. You gave me reason to believe in my words. You shined light down my tunnel when I pretended to be blind. You are the ones I will keep close at heart. Oh, and thanks to those who pissed me off. Y'all gave me great content; the dragon has awoken.

xoxox, from the marvelously magnificent, Brianna Florian

YOU can learn more about Brianna on

WhoseThoughtAnyway.com

19614716R00091

Made in the USA
San Bernardino, CA
31 December 2018